Meet Mindy

This book is dedicated to my nieces and nephews, who continuously remind me of how much there is still to learn and pass on. —S.S.

Please visit our web site at: www.garethstevens.com
For a free color catalog describing Gareth Stevens Publishing's list of
high-quality books and multimedia programs, call 1-800-542-2595 (USA)
or 1-800-387-3178 (Canada). Gareth Stevens Publishing's fax: (414) 332-3567.

Library of Congress Cataloging-in-Publication Data

Secakuku, Susan.
    Meet Mindy / by Susan Secakuku; with photographs by John Harrington. — North American ed.
        p. cm. — (My world: Young Native Americans today)
    Originally published: Meet Mindy: a native girl from the Southwest. Hillsboro, OR: National Museum
of the American Indian, Smithsonian Institution, in association with Beyond Words Pub., © 2003, in series:
My world: Young Native Americans today.
    Summary: Details a day in the life of an Arizona girl of Hopi descent, looking at her family, the history of her tribe,
and some traditional ceremonies and customs that are still observed today.
        ISBN 0-8368-3794-0 (lib. bdg.)
    1. Secakuku, Melinda Susan, 1987—Juvenile literature.   2. Secakuku, Susan—Juvenile literature.   3. Hopi Indians—
Juvenile literature.   4. Hopi Indians—Biography—Juvenile literature.   5. Tewa Indians—Juvenile literature.
[1. Secakuku, Melinda Susan, 1987- .   2. Secakuku, Susan.   3. Hopi Indians—Biography.   4. Tewa Indians—
Biography.   5. Indians of North America—Arizona Biography.]   I. Harrington, John, 1966- , ill.   II. Title.   III. Series.
E99.H7S348   2003
305.897'45—dc21   2003045775

This edition first published in 2004 by
Gareth Stevens Publishing
A World Almanac Education Group Company
330 West Olive Street, Suite 100
Milwaukee, Wisconsin 53212 USA

Contemporary photos, unless otherwise noted, copyright © 2003 John Harrington (Siletz) and National
Museum of the American Indian, Smithsonian Institution. Text and other photos, unless otherwise noted,
copyright © 2003 Smithsonian Institution. First published in 2002 by Beyond Words Publishing, Inc.,
Hillsboro, Oregon. This edition published in 2004 by Gareth Stevens, Inc.

Project Director and Head of Publications, NMAI: Terence Winch
Series Editor, NMAI: Amy Pickworth
Designer: Andrea L. Boven, Boven Design Studio, Inc.
Gareth Stevens cover design: Melissa Valuch

Printed in the United States of America

1 2 3 4 5 6 7 8 9 07 06 05 04 03

The National Museum of the American Indian, Smithsonian Institution, is dedicated to working in collaboration
with the indigenous peoples of the Americas to protect and foster Native cultures throughout the Western
Hemisphere. The museum's publishing program seeks to augment awareness of Native American beliefs and
lifeways, and to educate the public about the history and significance of Native cultures.

The museum's George Gustav Heye Center in Manhattan opened in 1994; its Cultural Resources Center opened
in Suitland, Maryland, in 1998; and in 2004, the museum will open its primary facility on the National Mall in
Washington, D.C.

For information about the National Museum of the American Indian, visit the NMAI website at
www.AmericanIndian.si.edu.

Meet Mindy

A Native Girl from the Southwest

Susan Secakuku

with photographs by
John Harrington

My World: Young Native Americans Today

National Museum of the American Indian
Smithsonian Institution

Gareth Stevens Publishing
A WORLD ALMANAC EDUCATION GROUP COMPANY

Pay loloma I kwatsimú (pronounced bai LOW-low-ma ee KWA-tsee-muh). This means "Hello, my friends" in Hopi. My name is Susan Secakuku. I am Hopi, from the village of Supawlovi (pronounced suh-PAUL-oh-vee), and I am of the Butterfly Clan. The Hopi people have lived in northern Arizona for thousands of years. We are one of twenty-one different tribes located in the state of Arizona, and all of them are unique.

Until recently, I worked for the National Museum of the American Indian in Washington, D.C., helping Native peoples from across the United States, Canada, and South America get the information they need to set up and run their own museums and cultural centers. Now I have returned to my home, where I still work for museums, cultural centers, and other programs—both for my Hopi community and for other Native tribes throughout the United States.

The word Hopi means "Peaceful People." Most of our villages are on top, or at the foot, of three plateaus at the southern end of Black Mesa, located a few hours east of the Grand Canyon. The plateaus are known as First Mesa, Second Mesa, and Third Mesa. Each mesa has three or more Hopi villages, and each village has its own history. All the villages speak different dialects of the Hopi language. The people in Hano village speak a language that is completely different from Hopi, a language known as Tewa (pronounced TAY-wah).

The Hopi have lived there a long time. In fact, Oraibi (pronounced or-RYE-bee), located on Third Mesa, was founded sometime before 1150 A.D., making it the oldest, most continuously inhabited town in the United States.

Before Europeans started arriving in Arizona in the 1500s, Hopi people farmed, raised families, and practiced our traditional religion. Homes were constructed from sandstone, a mixture of mud and sand. Sandstone homes were built next to, or on top of, each other, like apartment buildings, with a central plaza for gatherings or ceremonies. Our society is matrilineal, meaning that we trace back our families and pass on our culture through the women. Traditionally, men own livestock and fruit trees, which they cultivate on land owned communally by their clans. Hopi women own the houses in the villages and everything within them. These things are passed down from mother to daughter.

OPPOSITE TOP: This photo shows Second Mesa. Susan's village, Supawlovi, is on the left, and Musangnovi (pronounced muh-SANG-no-vee) is on the right.

OPPOSITE MIDDLE: A map of the three mesas. (BASED ON A MAP FROM THE *HANDBOOK OF NORTH AMERICAN INDIANS, VOLUME 9*, COURTESY OF THE SMITHSONIAN NATIONAL MUSEUM OF NATURAL HISTORY).

OPPOSITE BOTTOM: A photo taken in the late 1800s of the two villages in the top photo, shown from a different angle. Historically, Hopi people built their homes on top of one another. Some homes may have had stairs inside, but usually the only way up or down was by ladder. Ladders were also easy to remove in case of invaders. (NMAI P18234)

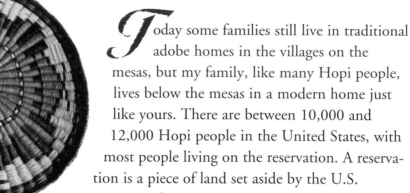

oday some families still live in traditional adobe homes in the villages on the mesas, but my family, like many Hopi people, lives below the mesas in a modern home just like yours. There are between 10,000 and 12,000 Hopi people in the United States, with most people living on the reservation. A reservation is a piece of land set aside by the U.S. government for a tribe. The original Hopi reservation was established in 1885 and since then has been made smaller. Today our reservation includes about 1.2 million acres of land, more than the entire state of Rhode Island.

For thousands of years, the Hopi have survived in a desert environment—hot temperatures in the summer and very little rain. Hopi men were and are talented farmers, though. Despite the heat and lack of water, they were able to grow squash, pumpkins, melons, different kinds of beans, and corn of many different colors. They also hunted deer, elk, and rabbits, wove traditional clothing from cotton and wool, and made buckskin shoes. Hopi women spent a lot of time preserving foods, cooking, maintaining the home, and rearing children. They also hauled all the water their families would need from the springs located near the mesa. This was a lot of work. Women made beautiful baskets and pottery from the plants and natural clays found in the area, too.

Today, some men and women still weave cloth and baskets, make pottery, and farm, usually in addition to working at regular jobs. Besides going to school, some Hopi kids learn to do these things, too.

Each Hopi person is born into his or her mother's clan, which, for me, means all my sisters (I have five of them!), my mother, my mother's brother and sisters, and my maternal grandmother are also of the Butterfly Clan. There are twelve Hopi villages and at least thirty different clans. Each clan has its own history and story that only its members know. Each clan also has a different role in Hopi ceremonial life. A person's role in Hopi life is based on age, whether they are male or female, the clan they were born into, and other societies that they may join through initiation. All Hopi clans are important and contribute to Hopi society.

TOP: Susan's father, Ferrell Secakuku, checks his corn plants at the beginning of harvest time. Hopi farmers plant corn much deeper in the soil and further apart than farmers in other regions do. This allows the plant to grow more extensive root systems and absorb more water from deeper underground.

BOTTOM: This corn, just harvested, is set out to dry. Once it is dried, shucked, and roasted, it can be ground into cornmeal. The husks are used for making special Hopi foods.

OPPOSITE: Baskets like this, called *yungyapu* (pronounced yung-YAH-buh), are made only by the women of the Third Mesa villages.

*T*he butterfly is important to Hopi society because in a dry climate where water is very precious, the butterfly's ability to locate water easily is a great gift. Butterfly Clan members are cheerful, friendly people who can lift people's spirits when they are sad, and calm them down when they are anxious or upset.

Like many other Hopi today, I was born and raised on the reservation within the Hopi culture and religion. Now I live away from home, but I go back to visit when I can, especially for the *katsina* (pronounced kat-SEE-nah) dances held in the summer. My niece, Mindy Secakuku, lives with her family near Phoenix, Arizona—only a few hours' drive from our village, and close enough for her to go home to Hopi often, sometimes for long periods of time.

Mindy is spending a lot of time on the reservation this summer. It's an important period for her, because she is taking steps to prepare for the next stage of her Hopi life, but I'll let her tell you about it.

OPPOSITE: This butterfly sculpture in the traditional Hopi style is a modern version of a katsina carving. You'll learn more about katsina dolls later in this book.

Loloma. My name is Mindy, and I'm fourteen. My Hopi name is Dawayumsi (pronounced dah-WAH-yum-see), which means "new dawn" or "beginning of a new day." I was given this name by my godmother, Colleen, in a special naming ceremony when I was initiated into the katsina society. My dad is an electrician and my mom is an analyst for a consulting firm. I have an older brother, Melvin. He's not too bad most of the time, but he likes to pick on me when Mom and Dad aren't around. His Hopi name is Suswupa (pronounced SUSS-woo-bah), which means "tallest bamboo." My grandmother, our dad's mom, gave him his name during his baby naming ceremony. Mom, Melvin, and I are of the Sand Clan. Sand is very important. It takes in seeds and nurtures new plant life, such as corn (which is used in almost all Hopi ceremonies), melons, beans, and squash. Sand is also the main source of the clay used by Hopi potters, and it is used in baby naming ceremonies. The horned toad and lizard are symbols of our clan. My dad is of the Reed Clan.

I was born in Germany when my dad was stationed there in the Army. I don't remember too much about Germany, but from what our mom tells us, Melvin and I were very mischievous! We moved back to Arizona when I was almost two years old.

My real home is my family's village, Tewa, also called Hano (pronounced HA-noh). It's one of three villages that make up First Mesa. The other two villages are Walpi (pronounced WALL-pee) and Sitchomovi (pronounced see-CHO-moe-vee). Another community located on the mesa below these villages is called Polacca (pronounced poe-LAH-kah).

My village's role in assisting the Hopi people is important to Hopi history. Many enemy attacks occurred during the 1600s, and during this time, Walpi village was besieged by enemy tribes who stole food, horses, and women. The Hopis decided to ask the Hano, or Tewa, people for help. The Tewa people were known as fearless warriors, and after several requests from the Hopi, they made the long journey to help them. The Tewa warriors fought many battles and finally won, and as a token of their appreciation, the Hopis invited the Tewa to live with them.

Today, the descendants of the Tewa warriors are the Tewa people of Hano. Tewa is also the name of a language spoken in my village and by the people of several pueblo tribes. The Tewa still live in Hano village, speaking their own language as well as Hopi. Because they have lived together for so long, the Tewa and Hopi are close, although their languages are very different. There are a lot of marriages between Hopi and Tewa people, but the Tewa have kept some of their own customs. My mom is Tewa, and my dad is Hopi. Although I understand both languages a little bit, we speak mostly English at home.

This is a very special year for me. Not only did I just start high school, but I have also been very involved in many Hopi and Tewa ceremonies and dances this summer. The most important event was my Corn Grinding Ceremony, which happened in early July. This is the traditional Hopi ceremony that prepares young women for marriage and motherhood—not that I'm ready to get married quite yet! But in our culture, the ability to give life is sacred, and as we get older and develop that power and responsibility, it is important to spend some time thinking about this.

The Corn Grinding Ceremony lasted five days and was held at my grandma's (my father's mom's) house. My aunts and grandmother were there to encourage me, but I was left alone most of the time, quietly spending the first four days using the traditional *mata* (pronounced MAH-tah) and *matàaki* (pronounced mah-TAH-kee), or grinding stone, to crush the hard corn kernels into fine cornmeal. It's hard work, making cornmeal. My arms were sore! But because Hopi women for many generations have also performed this ceremony, it felt very special for me to do it, too. Each day, I prayed hard that I would have the strength to do well.

During the four days, I wasn't allowed to eat any meat, salt, or fat, or to spend time with any male members of my family. Only women were allowed into Grandma's house. On the fifth day, my aunts and grandmother taught me how to make *piki* (pronounced BEE-kee) and *somiviki* (pronounced soh-MEE-vee-kee). These are special breads made with Hopi blue cornmeal. My aunts and grandmother also spent time talking with me about what it means to be a mature young Hopi woman, my new responsibilities as a young adult member of my clan, and how I'll be expected to act.

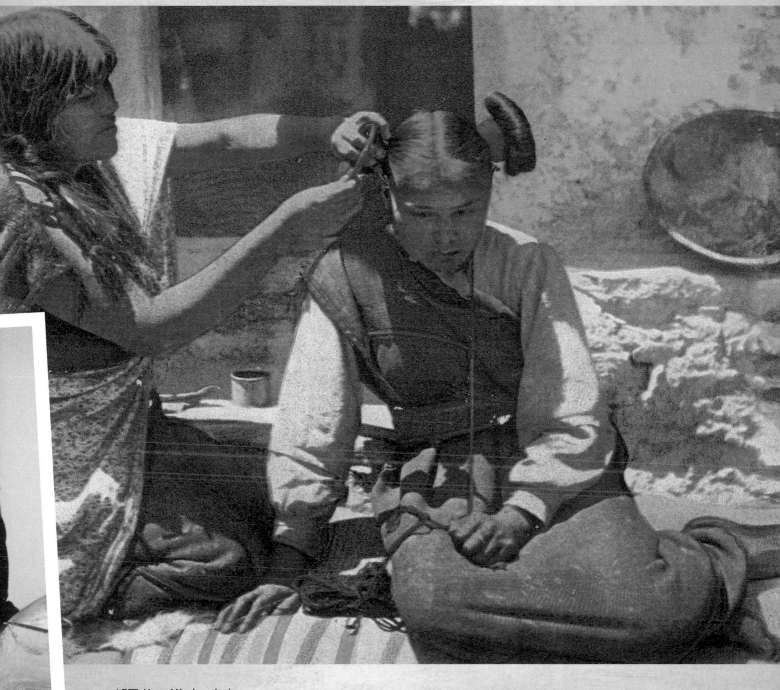

LEFT: Here Mindy grinds corn. (COURTESY OF THE SECAKUKU FAMILY)

ABOVE: This photo shows a Hopi girl about Mindy's age having her hair fixed. It was probably taken in the early 1900s. (NMAI P11669)

At the end of the last day, before I left my grandma's house, I went through a purification ceremony, which included a ritual hair washing. Then some of my hair was cut and the rest was styled into the traditional Hopi squash-blossom hairdo, which is only worn by unmarried women. On my way home, I walked through my village. The people who saw me wished me well, and the men said a special prayer for me to live a long and healthy life and to have a good marriage and strong children. When I got to my mother's house, she was there to greet me with my grandmother and aunts. Then the men in my family joined us for a feast.

Now I'm a young woman in Hopi society, and I'm expected to help more, to be more responsible, and to continue to learn more about Hopi traditions and my clan.

OPPOSITE TOP: On the fifth day of the Corn Grinding Ceremony, Mindy's aunts (Susan's sisters) Debbie and Bonnie help her with the purification ceremony and then dust her face with cornmeal.

OPPOSITE BOTTOM: This picture was taken just before Mindy walked home to her mother's house through her village. In the bundle she is holding are the piki and somiviki breads she made.

(BOTH PHOTOS COURTESY OF THE SECAKUKU FAMILY)

ack home in Glendale, Arizona, I've just started high school, another important part of growing up. I'm a freshman at Deer Valley High School, where I'm taking algebra, English, biology, computer applications, and ceramics.

Melvin and I have to wake up very early to get ready for school, then we walk there together. My life at school is pretty much like everyone else's. I'm hoping to make the girls' basketball team, though!

Getting ready for school.

Mindy's day at school probably looks a lot like yours.

OPPOSITE TOP: Walking to school with her brother, Melvin.

OPPOSITE BOTTOM: In biology class with her friend Karin Milton.

Although I am a regular American kid, I am a Hopi and Tewa kid first. Spirituality is very important to us, and our traditional religion is woven into our everyday lives. We believe that life is sacred, and that it is important to preserve and cherish life and be good to other people. This is true whether you live on the reservation or far away. My grand-father once told me, "You may call the house you live in at Glendale 'home,' but remember that your heart is here at Hopi." The Tewa still have their own ceremonies, but they mostly share the Hopi religion and lifestyle.

Since the beginning of life, the Hopi have believed that there have been a series of different worlds. We are now living in the Fourth World. The Fifth World, which some say is about to begin, will come after a period of evil and turmoil, and only people with good hearts will be left to carry on. The Hopi and Tewa try to live their lives very carefully. For us, one of the worst things you can do is to be selfish and think only of yourself. Bad behavior asks for punishment from the gods and could hurt you, or, worse yet, other people—even those who are innocent. For the good of the community, it is important that everyone try his or her best to live a good life, and to be humble, peaceful, grateful, and respectful. This includes respecting your elders.

Hopi kids are taught many important things by their parents and grandparents. Mindy has learned a lot about pottery from her grandmother, Verla Dewakuku, a talented potter. Nampeyo (Tewa, 1860–1942) was also a potter who lived in Hano village, and the pottery she made is famous today. Here Nampeyo (pronounced Nam-PAY-oh) is making pots with her own granddaughter, just like Mindy's grandmother sometimes does with her. (NMAI P18887)

The pot on the opposite page, from the collection of the National Museum of the American Indian, was made by Nampeyo's granddaughter, Rachel Nampeyo (1902–1985). Its wide, low shape is often seen in Hopi ceramics, and the bold designs, painted in red and black, are typical. (NMAI 21.2682)

We believe that there is one Creator who made all living things, but we also pray to other deities, or gods. The *katsinam* (pronounced kat-SEE-num) are deities that visit the Hopi people for six months of the year. We pray to the katsinam and ask them for rain, a good harvest, and a healthy, long, happy life. The Hopi traditional religion is the main religion of most Hopi people today, but a small number of people practice Western religions.

There are more than one hundred different kinds of katsinam, and each plays a different role during ceremonies. Some are guardians, some are leaders and chiefs, and others discipline everyone, reminding them to live good lives. These last katsinam are the ogres, and they are scary! Hopi kids are afraid even to look at them. Then there are clowns, such as the mudheads, who make us laugh and feel cheerful. Katsinam will bring us rain, happiness, and tranquility through our prayers to them. All the things we ask from them, though, are dependent on how we live our lives. We need to live good lives for them to help us.

The katsinam bring gifts to children who have been good. These gifts can be fruit or other food, or musical instruments like rattles, drums, or dancing sticks. A katsina may give a girl a very special gift of a miniature doll that looks like it, called *tíhu* (pronounced DEE-hu). You know you've been good when you get a katsina doll! These gifts help kids learn about the different kinds of katsinam and their purposes.

OPPOSITE: Mindy's father carves a katsina. Beside him is a finished doll.

In today's Hopi culture, dolls are still used as teaching tools and gifts, but some are also a source of income for Hopi artists because they are beautiful and are collected by tourists. My father and grandfather are Hopi katsina doll carvers, and it makes me sad and angry that many imitation katsina dolls are made by non-Hopi people who just want to make money. I know how much time and effort my dad and grandfather put into each katsina doll they carve. They also know what each doll represents and its role in Hopi ceremonies, and they understand the specific markings, colors, and clothing that are unique to each being. It may take them many days to complete one katsina doll, while hundreds of imitations are produced every day, usually by non-Hopi people. It seems very unfair when these fake dolls are said to be "authentic" or "genuine," especially when their makers don't understand their history or meaning.

ABOVE: The doll in Mindy's grandfather's right hand is of an eagle. Eagles symbolize security and strength. The doll in his left hand is of Red Beard Long Hair, a katsina who is especially powerful in bringing rain.

LEFT: These are the katsina dolls that Mindy received as gifts when she was a little girl. Her family has them on display in their house.

OPPOSITE RIGHT: This painting by Leroy Kewamyama (Hopi, b. 1922) is titled *Mudhead and Corn Katsina.* The mudhead katsina is on the left. (NMAI T237518)

L. KEWAMYAMA
HOPI

*L*ate summer is a time to celebrate the upcoming harvest, and one way of celebrating is dancing. Social dances are not as sacred as some other rituals, but they are still religious because the songs and dances are prayers. Some social dances honor other Native cultures we have relationships with through trade or shared history. These dances usually take place in the late summer, just before harvest. The Yah-ne-wah (pronounced YAH-nee-wah) Dance is a Tewa dance performed at Hano each August. It's also still practiced in Santa Clara Pueblo, where my Tewa ancestors originally came from.

Families take turns sponsoring dances, and my family is hosting one this year. It's a lot of work to sponsor a dance. As a female dancer, I provide the food for my partner. But our family also needs to make food for all the men who are helping us with the dance—the singers, those who pray for the dancers, and those who provide tobacco and other materials used for the dance. We will also feed all the dancers and singers the day of the dance. Because it's so much work, we'll go back to Hopi before the weekend so that my mom and I can help my grandma and other women in my family cook and bake.

OPPOSITE TOP: This black-and-white photo, taken in 1919, shows the Butterfly Dance in progress. Notice the fancy headdress worn by the girl in the front on the right. In the background you can see lots of people from the village standing on the roofs of the houses so they can get a better look at the dance. (NMAI N28241)

OPPOSITE BOTTOM: This picture shows Mindy dressed for the Zuni-style Butterfly Dance (without her headdress).

Another social dance held in late summer is the Butterfly Dance. Each girl gets to choose a male partner, and once chosen, he designs and makes an elaborate headdress for her. These headdresses are beautiful and unique, and they are a very special gift.

A celebration of the upcoming harvest, the Butterfly Dance is a time to strengthen clan relationships and includes several days of feasting. The men of the village sing songs about rain, harvest, and happiness as the whole village participates by watching.

*W*e drive out to Hopi after school on Thursday. Since the school year has started, my mom has to excuse me for a couple of days for the preparation. I think it's kind of fun not being in class, but Mom always makes sure I get my assignments! It's a four-hour drive to Hano village, but it doesn't seem that long to me. We go there a lot, and Melvin and I bring CDs and magazines to entertain ourselves in the car. Along the way, we go through Flagstaff, at the base of Nuvatukya'ovi (pronounced nu-VAH-tuh-kya-oh-vee), also known as the San Francisco Peaks. This is the spiritual home of the katsinam, and where they live until they are summoned by the Hopi. We also drive across a lot of the Navajo reservation, because the Hopi reservation is located in the middle of it.

The Hopi have lived here a very long time, and it is only very recently that we became neighbors with the Navajo tribe. We are very different peoples, but when the U.S. government created reservations, they usually did not take these kinds of distinctions into account. They also didn't use the original boundaries that most tribes had accepted for a long time, and this has sometimes made things difficult for the tribes. The Navajo reservation now includes much of what was the Hopi land, and this has created disagreements between the Hopi and Navajo about who owns the land and how it should be used. Today the Hopi reservation lies in the middle of the Navajo reservation.

We have to stop for gas, and sometimes Mom lets Melvin and me get snacks like soda, chips, or candy. Not today, though, because we're having dinner with my grandparents when we get to their house this evening. They live on First Mesa, in a house near the plaza. My mom and her sisters and brother grew up in this house, and my grandmother before them, and so on. Our family has lived here for a very long time.

It's peaceful on the mesa. Sometimes you hear a dog bark or the sounds of somebody's radio, but mostly it's quiet.

ABOVE: The Hopi name for these hills is Löhavutsostmo (pronounced loo-HA-vuh-tsost-moh). They are made up of cinder from an ancient volcanic eruption.

*T*he next morning is *totokya* (pronounced doh-DOH-kya), the name for the day before a big ceremony. I wake up early to help start mixing dough for the apple and cherry pies. We need to make lots of them!

The women in my family are in the kitchen speaking in Tewa and laughing. Yesterday they made piki, the flat bread made from blue cornmeal. Today Aunt Iva is cooking hominy, or corn kernels that have been boiled until they are soft. My grandfather is out back cutting up lamb for our traditional lamb and hominy stew, called *nöqkwivi* (pronounced NULCK-kwee-vee) in Hopi, or *dusala* (pronounced duh-SAH-lah) in Tewa. My little cousins are playing quietly in the front room.

We make thirty-two pies, and we bake them all at once in the adobe oven behind the house. It's important to get the oven's temperature just right, and although it's not her favorite task, Aunt Iva gets it ready for baking and I help her. This method of baking has been used by Hopi women for many, many generations. A mound of firewood is placed in the middle of the oven, and then is set on fire. As it burns, the inside walls of the oven are watched closely, and when they've turned a whitish color, the oven is ready. The ashes are swept out, the pies are placed inside with a long paddle, and the front of the oven is sealed off. In about an hour, the pies are ready. Yum! After we're finished making pies and more bread and other pastries, we clean up, and I make sure that I have my outfit ready for the dance tomorrow.

ABOVE and LEFT: Mindy makes pies with, from left in the top photo, her mother, Camelia Secakuku; her grandmother, Verla Dewakuku; and Tanya Mahle, her clan niece.

Mindy's grandfather, Daniel Dewakuku, cuts up lamb.

Social dances are a special time for Hopi girls. Only the young, unmarried, and childless girls of the village participate. Dances celebrate the purity of young women, and some of the female dancers are only five or six years old. Your choice of dance partner is based on your clan relationship. A girl can dance only with a male whose father is of the same clan as she is. In my case, I can only dance with a boy whose father is of the Snake or Sand Clans. (The Snake Clan and Sand Clan have a close relationship, so they are considered nearly the same.) The rest of the village also participates—most of the men and young boys not chosen to dance will sing, and everyone else watches.

When this year's Ya-ne-wah Dance was announced, I knew I wanted to participate. I talked to my mom about choosing Pernell Mahle, whom we all call Budge, as my partner. Two weeks before the dance, we began practicing every night, learning the songs and perfecting the steps. On the night before the dance, everyone who is dancing or singing is expected to stay up the entire night. This helps to purify our minds and hearts. At about 10 P.M., the chaperone comes to collect me and all the other female dancers, and we go to the *kiva* (pronounced KEE-vah), an underground room built under the village plaza and used for special ceremonies. Kivas are holy places, so we don't take photographs inside them, but some have beautiful paintings on the walls and are large enough to hold a hundred people. The singers and our partners also arrive at the kiva, and we spend the next six hours practicing. At about 3 A.M., when everyone starts to get really sleepy, the dancers all return home to pick up the evening meal, and then we meet back at the kiva. Like all the partners, Budge brings the main dinner, and I, as the girl, bring pastries, and we eat together. As dawn approaches, every person participating in the dance leaves the kiva to greet the sun with special prayers.

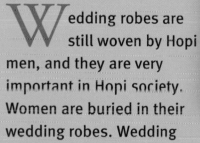

Wedding robes are still woven by Hopi men, and they are very important in Hopi society. Women are buried in their wedding robes. Wedding robes are sort of like magic carpets for Hopi souls and transport them into the next world after death. All traditional Hopi marriage ceremonies take time to prepare for and involve four phases, which may take years to complete. Often children are born and raised before the ceremony is completed. A civil or other religious marriage ceremony usually precedes a traditional Hopi ceremony. The picture was taken several years ago at the Hopi wedding of Mindy's parents, Scott and Camelia. It includes Mindy and Melvin when they were younger. Cornmeal has been dusted on their faces, a ritual that is part of many Hopi ceremonies. (COURTESY OF THE SECAKUKU FAMILY)

The second picture, taken in Oraibi many years ago, shows another Hopi woman dressed in her wedding robe. As you can see, the style of traditional clothing hasn't really changed. (NMAI P15975)

*I*n the Yah-ne-wah Dance, only four pairs of dancers perform at a time. Budge and I aren't dancing until this afternoon, so we have some time to wait before that. Melvin is dancing this afternoon, too. We spend the time in the plaza watching the other dancers and playing with our little cousins.

Finally, it's time to start getting ready. Before I dance, I put on my Tewa dress (a cotton dress with long sleeves), a Hopi belt, and buckskin shoes. Then I pick out my scarf, bracelet, earrings, and rings, and make sure my shoes are clean. These traditional Hopi and Tewa shoes are worn only by women. Long pieces of white buckskin hide are wrapped tightly around the lower legs so that the shoes do not come undone during the dance. Buckskin shoes are thick and can also get very hot.

After we're dressed, the dancers are taken back to the kiva, where we finish putting on the rest of the dance ornaments, and our hands and faces are painted. You can sometimes tell the girls who have already danced today, because they often still have red circles on their cheeks.

OPPOSITE: Family friend Tina Neil combs Mindy's hair.

RIGHT BOTTOM: Mindy's cousin, Denise Namingha, helps Mindy wrap buckskin hide tightly around her leg.

Everyone gathers in the Hano village plaza, on First Mesa, for the dances.

As with many Hopi ceremonies, this dance is about rain and our prayers for a good harvest. It also gives people a chance to come together to spread cheer and pray for each other.

The lyrics we sing, the clothes and ornaments we wear, and the gestures we make during the dance are all very important. We sing about weather and the rain, and our hopes for good health, long life, and happiness. The painted basket I'm carrying symbolizes the sun, and the dyed red animal hair suggests the sun's rays. The brightly colored feathers in my hair and behind my head are like the beautiful flowers the rains can bring us. In the middle of the dance, the male dancers dip and lunge toward us with their sticks, which represent lightning, while the other female dancers and I kneel, swishing our baskets back and forth, like we're sweeping the rain into the fields so the plants can drink it up.

During the dance, Budge's family gives me some presents to thank me for choosing their son as my partner. I also may get a few dollars as gifts. After the dance, we take a little bit of the money we made and walk to the store around the corner from the plaza to buy pickles or snowcones.

OPPOSITE LEFT: Mindy's grand-mother gives her a gift during the dance, which Mindy will in turn give to her partner.

Later that day, when the dances are finished, we relax at my grandparents' house. I feel tired, but also good. It is really fun to dance. From the practicing to the baking to the actual performance, it has been a lot of work, but it's very rewarding. I'm very proud that I danced today, and I appreciate all the hard work my family has done to allow me to do this.

Later tonight Melvin and I are going with our friends to the football game at Hopi High School. It will be a lot of fun, and hopefully we'll win. It's the homecoming game.

A Hopi Year

The Hopi people have their own calendar. It has been around for a very long time. Our calendar focuses on the ceremonial and religious responsibilities and activities that occur throughout the year. It also helps us know when to plant and harvest, and when we should think about our personal goals and growth for the year. Activities within the Hopi year also help us remember our ancient history and serve as a reminder for us to live good and productive lives, to be grateful and good to one another, and, most of all, to try to achieve peace.

The sun and the moon play important parts in measuring Hopi time. The Hopi calendar is based on the cycles of the moon, so, like the modern calendar, there are twelve months, each with its own name and general purpose. The equinoxes and solstices also play important roles, and the winter solstice in particular is a time when all are reminded of how precious life is. This calendar is still used by Hopi people today, but we also use the modern calendar in our jobs and at school.

Let's look at the Hopi year together.

WINTER

The winter season is a time for traditional Hopi weddings. Kelmuya (pronounced KEL-muh-yah), in November, is when the Hopi new year begins. The men who are involved in certain levels of the Hopi religion purify their minds and spirits with special ceremonies. This is the beginning of the religious cycle.

Kyaamuya (pronounced KYA-muh-yah) occurs in December, and marks a quiet time for thinking about the many spiritual forces at work in our world. Myths and stories of the past are told during this time to give us moral guidance. The winter solstice also occurs during this month, which allows for each person to reflect on his or her growth, goals, and desires for the year.

Paamuya (pronounced BAH-muh-yah), in January, is a time for winter social dances, such as the Buffalo Dance. This is a festive period filled with dances celebrating animals that live in snowy regions. These dances pray for snow on Hopi fields or for successful hunting.

Powamuya (pronounced BOH-wah-muh-yah) happens in February, with ceremonies of the katsinam, or spirit beings. In the Bean Dance, the katsinam will present special bean sprouts and other foods that suggest the upcoming planting season. We are told that the katsinam have been watching us to judge our conduct, and if it has been good, Hopi boys will be rewarded with special gifts of rattles and Hopi girls will get katsina dolls or dancing sticks. This is also when traditional Hopi wedding engagements are made. A purification ceremony by the ogre katsinam also happens this month, when everyone in the village—children and adults—is publicly ridiculed and punished for not living as carefully as he or she should have. Special healing blessings are then given to carry us forward.

SPRING

March brings Ösömuya (pronounced oh-SO-muh-yah), when the katsinam arrive to dance late at night in the underground ceremonial rooms called kivas. The katsinam bring gifts of fruit, corn, and sweets, and their dances include songs that pray for happiness for all life. Children are asked to take naps before the dances so they will not fall asleep. The spring equinox occurs this month, beginning the twenty-one-day countdown to the planting of early corn.

The start of Kwiyamuya (pronounced KWEE-yah-muh-yah) is marked by the blossoming of the fruit trees in April. For young boys, this is also the time to help their fathers or grandfathers begin preparing the fields and building windbreaks so the first corn can be planted. Racer katsinam appear in the village to challenge the young males to footraces to test their strength, and the fertility spirit, Kokopölmana (pronounced ko-ko-POOL-ma-na), also comes, representing germination and new life. All this is meant to bless the people, and to encourage the men and boys for the upcoming planting season and enhance their strength.

SUMMER

In the month of Hakitonmuya (pronounced ha-KEE-don-muh-yah), which occurs in May, we continue to wait for warmer weather to plant the main crop of corn, although the men and boys do begin planting beans, pumpkin, watermelon, and gourds at this time. The men and boys of certain clans also collect eaglets and young hawks, which are adopted into the clan families and treated like their own. These birds will live on these families' rooftops all summer to observe and protect the people of the village.

Wuko'uyis (pronounced wuh-KOH-uh-yees), in June, is the month for planting corn. Throughout this month, the katsinam visit the Hopi people in the villages and dance and sing in the plaza. We pray to them for rain for the recently planted crops, for a good life, and for healing, and the katsinam give gifts of food, which are samples of the upcoming harvest. This month is the summer solstice, and a certain number of days after it occurs, some girls will have their puberty ceremonies, or Corn Grindings.

Talangva (pronounced DAHL-ang-vah) happens in July. Katsina dances continue this month as the men and boys maintain the fields and keep them free of weeds. The climax of the summer is the Home Dance, the final katsina dance of the season. The girls who have just undergone their puberty ceremonies and the brides who were married in traditional Hopi wedding ceremonies during the past winter are presented at the Home Dance. Young girls may also receive katsina dolls at this dance. The men meditate and pray hard to send the katsinam back to their spiritual home, and this concludes the katsina season.

Taala'vamuya (pronounced da-LAH-vaa-muh-yah), in August, is the time for the Flute and Snake Dances. These dances occur in alternate years and bring the last of the summer rains, which help the corn crop finish growing and nourish wild plants and animals. Social dances, such as the colorful Butterfly Dance, begin this month, as well as dances that honor other tribes, such as the Navajo, Havasupai, Zuni, and Comanche. Younger Hopi kids participate a lot in these dances, which help celebrate the upcoming harvest and reinforce family and clan relations.

FALL

Nasanmuya (pronounced na-SAN-muh-yah), in September, marks the work of harvesting corn, which is usually done by the whole family. The women's religious society, which can also involve young girls, begins ceremonies this month.

In October is Tuho'osmuya (pronounced DUH-hoh-os-muh-yah), and the cycle of women's ceremonies continues. The Basket Dances celebrate motherhood and speak to the desire for healthy families and births. With the end of these ceremonies, the Hopi year comes to an end.